The Ed Emberley Connection

by Will C. Howell

FEARON TEACHER AIDS
Simon & Schuster Supplementary Education Group

Ed Emberley,

*Our first meeting was at a small-town library autographing that
was poorly publicized and sparsely attended. This gave me time to
visit with—or harass—you. When you asked me how to sign Klippity
Klop, I flippantly suggested, "To my close personal friend." That's
what you wrote. Thank you for your books and for your friendship.*

Will Howell

Editor: Carol Williams
Copyeditor: Kristin Eclov
Illustration: Gwen Connelly
Cover illustration: Reprinted from *Drummer Hoff* with the permission of
   Ed Emberley.
Design: Diann Abbott

ISBN 0-86653-975-1

Printed in the United States of America
1. 9 8 7 6 5 4 3 2 1

Contents

Introduction

The emphasis on "The Year of the Young Reader" (1989), "International Literacy Year" (1990), and "Year of the Lifetime Reader" (1991) has helped children's literature come of age. Research confirms that good reading and writing are best taught by using good books. And today, educators are fortunate to have a wide selection of excellent children's books to choose from.

The Ed Emberley Connection is written for librarians and teachers who want to effectively use good literature in their classrooms. The lessons present art, math, creative writing, reading, science, and social studies activities to accompany books by this one outstanding author/illustrator. The variety of interdisciplinary activities and the whole-language instructional approach incorporated in the lessons will help you meet the diverse needs and interests of your students.

While following the familiar format of the series, *The Ed Emberley Connection* is unique. In addition to activities to accompany Ed Emberley's award-winning literature books, you will find activities to accompany his imaginative drawing books. Another unique quality is the inclusion of several computer activities written by computer-education specialist, Janet N. Howell.

As students become familiar with various works by a single author/illustrator, they develop an ability to analyze literary and artistic styles. Children can go to the library and select books written or illustrated by authors they feel as if they have actually met. "Connecting" with authors stimulates students to become involved in and enthusiastic about reading, writing, and learning. *The Ed Emberley Connection* gives students the opportunity to meet an author/illustrator who has established himself in the fields of literature and art.

Lessons require minimal preparation, while resulting in maximum participation and learning. A brief synopsis of each book is included. Read the book aloud to the children and invite them to enjoy the illustrations before participating in the activities. Exciting activities, including "Turtle Walk," "Dragon Book," and "Ark-Itects," will help you to enhance and reinforce your curriculum.

Meet Ed Emberley

Ed Emberley was born on October 19, 1931 in Malden, Massachusetts.

When he was a boy, Ed and his two brothers were encouraged to draw by their parents who always kept paper and pencils handy in the house. Ed's parents and high school teachers encouraged him to attend the Massachusetts School of Art when he finished high school.

Ed married Barbara Emberley, whom he met at school. They were married a year after graduation.

Barbara has frequently joined forces with Ed on book projects, including text writing and color separation for the 1968 Caldecott winner, *Drummer Hoff*. The Emberley children, Rebecca and Michael, have also been closely involved with books. Both children are now authors themselves.

Ed and Barbara Emberley live in a 1690 saltbox house in Ipswich, Massachusetts. They jog, cross-country ski, sail, and continue to develop wonderful books for children.

Drummer Hoff

This cumulative rhyming verse describes a group of happy warriors who build a cannon that goes "kahbahbloom!" The intricate woodcut illustrations, which received a Caldecott Award in 1968, have captured and entertained children of all ages.

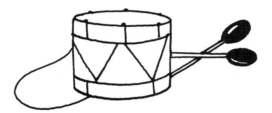

Adapted by Barbara Emberley
Illustrated by Ed Emberley
New York: Prentice-Hall, 1967

DRUMMER HOFF IN THE CLASSROOM

Materials:

- worksheet on page 9
- fairy tales
- lined paper
- pencils

Lesson Procedure

1. Inform students that you have access to the true story of *Drummer Hoff* and then read the story provided on page 9. Explain that this story is a take-off of the original, but takes place in a classroom setting.
2. Share some other interesting fairy tale take-offs, such as *Jack and the Beanstalk* by Steven Kellogg (New York: Morrow Junior Books, 1991), *Red Riding Hood* by James Marshall (New York: Dial Books for Young Readers, 1987), or *The True Story of the Three Little Pigs* by Jon Scieszka (New York: Viking Kestrel, 1989).
3. Invite students to select a fairy tale and rewrite it in a contemporary or unusual setting, such as a scout camp, cafeteria, school bus, space station, or jungle. Encourage students to tell the story from the point of view of a less-featured character.
4. Encourage each student to edit and rewrite his or her fairy tale on lined paper. Then combine the students' fairy tales into a class booklet and place in the library or reading center.

Taking It Further . . .

Invite students to sit in a circle. Begin with a starter sentence, such as "Lucy and Betty ate the spaghetti." Going around the circle, each student in turn adds to the story by contributing a rhyming couplet, such as "Sammy Otter boiled the water" or "Nancy and Walt added the salt." Be prepared with a list of suggestions if students are stumped.

The Story of Drummer Hoff in the Classroom

Once there was a rambunctious young man whose name was Gary Hoff. But no one called him Gary. Everyone called him Drummer because he was always tapping something. He tapped his pencil. He tapped his feet. He tapped his fingers. Drum. Drum. Drum. So he became known as Drummer Hoff.

Drumming was not Drummer Hoff's singular fault. He also fought, tipped back in his chair, and listened to music during class.

One day Drummer Hoff got caught wearing headphones in math class. Naturally, he gave the teacher, Mrs. Hildegard, an excuse.

"But Peter Parriage cranked up the volume!"

"Peter Parriage cranked up the volume, but Drummer Hoff didn't shut it off," said Mrs. Hildegard.

"But Corey Farrell turned on the music!"

"Corey Farrell turned on the music, Peter Parriage cranked up the volume, But Drummer Hoff didn't shut it off!" argued Mrs. Hildegard.

"But Archie Chowder put in the tape!"

"Archie Chowder put in the tape, Corey Farrell turned on the music, Peter Parriage cranked up the volume, But Drummer Hoff didn't shut it off!" demanded Mrs. Hildegard.

"Gabby Bammer brought the tape!"

"Gabby Bammer brought the tape, Archie Chowder put in the tape, Corey Farrell turned on the music, Peter Parriage cranked up the volume, But Drummer Hoff didn't shut it off!" insisted Mrs. Hildegard.

"Sandy Scott gave me the headphones!"

"Sandy Scott gave you the headphones, Gabby Bammer brought the tape, Archie Chowder put in the tape, Corey Farrell turned on the music, Peter Parriage cranked up the volume, But Drummer Hoff didn't shut it off!" maintained Mrs. Hildegard.

"Georgie Border said to do it!"

"Georgie Border said to do it, Sandy Scott gave you the headphones, Gabby Bammer brought the tape, Archie Chowder put in the tape, Corey Farrell turned on the music, Peter Parriage cranked up the volume, But Drummer Hoff didn't shut it off!" proclaimed Mrs. Hildegard.

KAHBAHBLOOM! blared the music.

The moral of the story is that everyone must shoulder his or her own blame.

CREATIVE WRITING

Materials:

•lined paper
•pencils

Lesson Procedure

1. Discuss the cumulative pattern in the story. Each time a new character is introduced, each preceding character is reviewed in reverse order.
2. Suggest new titles for stories that could be written to follow the same cumulative pattern.

Lucy and Betty Ate the Spaghetti
Mrs. Myrtle Found the Turtle

Dr. Star Drove the Car
Flying Ace Went into Space

3. Invite students to brainstorm a list of sequential steps for a new story, such as "Lucy and Betty Ate the Spaghetti." Write the suggestions on the chalkboard.

cook the meat
slice the tomatoes
add the spice.

boil noodles
sprinkle the cheese

4. As a class, encourage students to work cooperatively to turn each step into a rhyming couplet.

Joe from Barbados sliced the tomatoes.
Alice and Bryce added the spice.
Muff and Poodles boiled the noodles.

Ted and Louise sprinkled the cheese.
But Lucy and Betty ate the spaghetti.

5. Invite students to select themes and write stories independently or in small groups. Emphasize the importance of having the steps in the correct order so the story makes sense.

Taking It Further . . .

Students can illustrate their cumulative stories by drawing the sequential steps in order on a long piece of butcher paper.

♘ • CHARACTER SKETCH • ♘

Materials:

•worksheet on page 12
•pencils

Lesson Procedure

1. Take a closer look at each character in the story and ask students to make some inferences about them based on their actions or appearance. Invite students to be creative.

> Private Parriage has a crooked nose. Perhaps he was a fighter and it got broken.
> Sergeant Chowder has a peg leg. Perhaps he lost his leg in a famous battle.
> Captain Bammer has an eye patch. Perhaps he ran into a tree.

2. Have students select a character from *Drummer Hoff* and write a creative description of his background and habits.

Taking It Further . . .

Challenge students to use their character sketches to write a story. Suggest titles, such as "A Day in the Life of . . . ," "How I Got Where I Am Today," or "My Father, the Major."

Name _____

Character Sketch of

_____

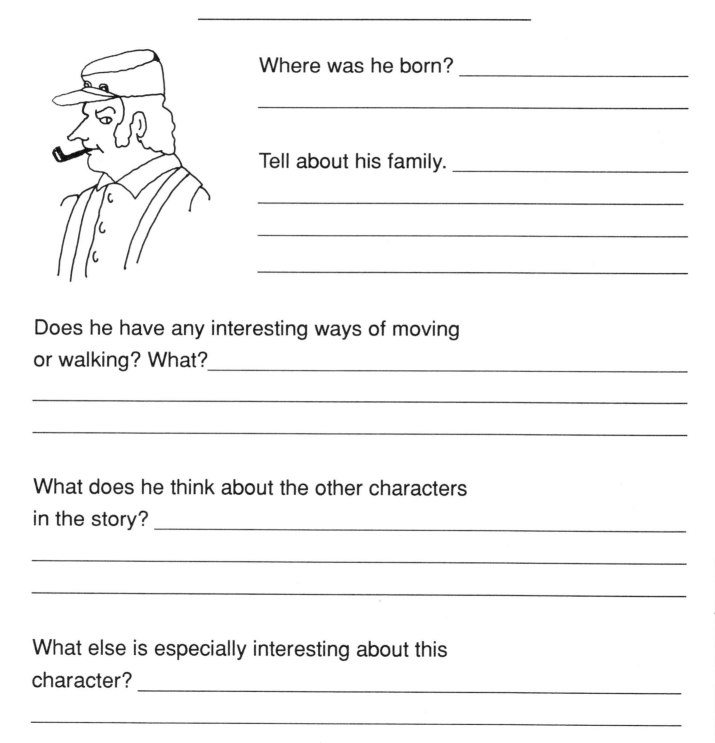

Where was he born? _____

_____

Tell about his family. _____

_____

_____

_____

Does he have any interesting ways of moving
or walking? What?_____

_____

_____

What does he think about the other characters
in the story? _____

_____

_____

What else is especially interesting about this
character? _____

_____

_____

The Ed Emberley Connection © 1992 Fearon Teacher Aids

Drummer Hoff

 **WAR AND PEACE**

Materials:

- lined paper
- pencils

Lesson Procedure

1. Discuss war as it is depicted in this book. Discussion stimulators might include the injuries to the characters or the end of the cannon overgrown with flowers.
2. Share books with similar themes.

   Asch, Frank and Vladimir Vagin. *Here Comes the Cat!* New York: Scholastic, 1989.
   Browne, Anthony. *The Tunnel*. New York: Alfred A. Knopf, 1989.
   Scholes, Katherine. *Peace Begins with You*. San Francisco:
       Little, Brown & Company, 1989.
   Seuss, Dr. *The Butter Battle Book*. New York: Random House, 1984.
   Durrel, Ann and Marilyn Sachs. *The Big Book for Peace*. New York: Dutton, 1990.

3. On the chalkboard, list ways individuals "make war." Discuss attitudes, comments, and actions, such as resentment, unkind words, or hitting.
4. On the chalkboard, list ways individuals "make peace." Discuss attitudes, comments, and actions, such as forgiveness, apologizing, and smiling.
5. Invite students to write stories that demonstrate peace and harmony.

Taking It Further . . .

Invite students to make peace posters. Encourage students to illustrate things they can do in the classroom, on the playground, and at home that will create peace, rather than hostility.

☙ • MILITARY HATS • ❧

Materials:

- •assorted art paper (construction, tissue, crepe)
- •assorted ribbon, yarn, beads, and glitter
- •scissors
- •glue
- •pencils

Lesson Procedure

1. Divide the class into seven groups. Assign each group a character from the story. Challenge each group to design a military hat for their character.

   Drummer Hoff   Private Parriage
   Corporal Farrell   Sergeant Chowder
   Captain Bammer   Major Scott
   General Border

2. Encourage students to work as a group and cooperatively decide upon and draw a hat design.
3. Using art supplies available in the classroom, students can construct hats for each member of the group.

Taking It Further . . .

Invite students to wear their hats to do a choral reading of *Drummer Hoff*. Each group can read the sentence about their character.

Ed Emberley's

Grasshoppers are golfing in the green and a bear builds a "B" from berries in a basket in this inventive alphabet book. Wild and crazy animals show how each letter is formed as they entertain with unusual antics.

Boston: Little, Brown & Company, 1978

ABC

◆• ABC BOOK REPORT •◆

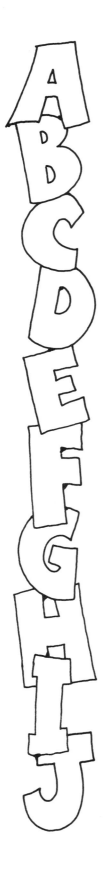

Materials:

- •lined paper
- •pencils

Lesson Procedure

1. Encourage each student to select a book for his or her report, then write the title, author, and illustrator of the book on a sheet of lined paper.
2. Have students write each letter of the alphabet on a separate line down the left-hand side of the paper. (Two sheets of paper may be necessary.)
3. Encourage students to write a word from their books that begins with each letter of the alphabet. Students can also write a sentence following each word that explains the meaning of the word or how it relates to the story. Here are some examples from *Charlotte's Web* by E.B. White.

   > A Avery—Fern's brother who liked to sleep in.
   > B Barn—Fern spent a lot of time in it.
   > C Charlotte—She was a smart spider.

Taking It Further . . .

Encourage primary students to make an ABC picturebook report. Students can write one word for each letter and draw an illustration instead of writing a sentence.

THE COST OF WORDS

Materials:

•worksheet on page 18
•pencils
•dictionaries
•lined paper
•calculators (optional)

Lesson Procedure

1. Hand out the worksheet on page 18 and discuss the money value of each letter. Demonstrate how $10.00 would be the total for the cost of the word *dog*.

    DOG $4.00 + $3.00 + $3.00 = $10.00

2. Practice calculating the cost of several other words as well.

    CAT $3.00 + $1.00 + $4.00 = $8.00
    ROBIN $2.00 + $3.00 + $2.00 + $1.00 + $2.00 = $10.00
    ELF $1.00 + $4.00 + $2.00 = $7.00
    CHAIR $3.00 + $4.00 + $1.00 + $1.00 + $2.00 = $11.00

3. On a separate sheet of paper, challenge students to write as many words as they can, spending a total of $100.00.
4. Have students star their most expensive word and circle their least expensive word. (All words must be at least three letters long.)
5. Challenge students to use reading books or dictionaries as they search for the most expensive word possible. Remind students that the most expensive word may not necessarily be the longest.

Taking It Further . . .

Challenge students to compute the cost of their spelling or vocabulary words. With primary students, use counters to help them with one-to-one correspondence.

Use the chart below to find out the price of each letter in the words provided. Add the letters together. On a separate sheet of paper, make as many words as you can for a total of $100.00.

$1.00	A	E	I	M	Q	U	Y
$2.00	B	F	J	N	R	V	Z
$3.00	C	G	K	O	S	W	
$4.00	D	H	L	P	T	X	

CAT $3.00 + $1.00 + $4.00 = $8.00

ROBIN   _____

ELF   _____

CHAIR   _____

The Ed Emberley Connection © 1992 Fearon Teacher Aids

Ed Emberley's ABC

◆ PARTS OF SPEECH ◆

Materials:

•worksheet on page 20
•pencils

Lesson Procedure

1. Discuss how Ed Emberley uses nouns, verbs, and adjectives to feature the letter on each page of the alphabet book.

   goose (noun)
   golf (verb)
   gray (adjective)

2. Hand out the worksheet and challenge students to work independently, in pairs, or in teams to find a word for each letter and part of speech. (Students may use words that end in the letter when finding words that begin with the letter is difficult.)

Taking It Further . . .

After students have completed most of the worksheet, invite them to create humorous alliterative sentences, paragraphs, or short stories using their word lists. For example, "Silly Suzy sat on a seesaw."

Parts of Speech

How many nouns, verbs, and adjectives can you think of that begin (or end) with each letter?

	Nouns	Verbs	Adjectives
A			
B			
C			
D			
E			
F			
G			
H			
I			
J			
K			
L			
M			
N			
O			
P			
Q			
R			
S			
T			
U			
V			
W			
X			
Y			
Z			

The Ed Emberley Connection © 1992 Fearon Teacher Aids

THE LAST LETTER

Materials:

• lined paper
• pencils

Lesson Procedure

1. Point out how Ed Emberley sometimes uses the last letter of a word to feature a certain letter—for the N page, he uses the words *lion, raccoon, ribbon,* and *green,* for example.
2. Challenge students to make a list of words alphabetically arranged by their last letters.
3. Have students write the alphabet down the right-hand side of a piece of lined paper. Students can fill in a word on each line that ends with the letter of the alphabet.
4. To make the activity more challenging, suggest that students use words that fit a category. For example, they might make a list of food words.

   A—banan<u>a</u>
   B—corn-on-the-co<u>b</u>
   C—bro<u>c</u>coli

5. Remind students that they may need to use the middle letter of some words, as with the letter "c" in broccoli.

Taking It Further . . .

Challenge students to think of other ways to alphabetize words as well. Ideas might include using the second letter of each word, the middle letter, or alternating patterns, such as a word beginning with A, a word ending with B, a word beginning with C, and so on.

❧• COLLAGE LETTERS •❧

Materials:

- •9" x 12" tagboard
- •pencils
- •glue
- •assorted collage materials, such as beads, corn, sand, eggshells, buttons, rocks, ribbons, fabric scraps, and yarn

Lesson Procedure

1. Invite each student to select a letter of the alphabet and a collage material that begins with that letter. For example, a student may choose to make the letter "B" using beans, the letter "C" using cord, or the letter "S" using sand.
2. Have students draw their chosen letter on tagboard.
3. Students can then use glue and the collage material they chose to outline or fill in the penciled letter.

Taking It Further . . .

After students have completed their collage letters, invite them to write stories using as many words as they can that begin with their chosen letter. A "B" story may begin, "A bear in Brookings came out of a big, black cave. She found a bush bursting with bright, blueberries for breakfast."

Ed Emberley's

Along with a host of Halloween drawings, Ed Emberley offers a wide variety of orange art ideas—orange fruit, orange tigers, orange carrots, and orange rabbits to eat them! The master challenge is to draw a marvelously spooky house.

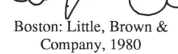

Boston: Little, Brown & Company, 1980

Big Orange Drawing Book

☙ · COMIC STRIP · ☙

Materials:

•worksheet on page 25
•pencils

Lesson Procedure

1. Give students opportunities to practice drawing characters from *Ed Emberley's Big Orange Drawing Book.*
2. Ask students to choose two characters from the book, such as Sniffer, Willum, Buttercup, or Schnider Spider, and use them to create a comic strip.
3. While using the worksheet for the cartoon format, remind students that the first two frames should introduce a problem. The last two frames should solve the problem. The middle two frames should guide the reader from the problem to the solution. Remind students to write what each character says in dialogue balloons.

Taking It Further . . .

To practice using quotation marks, instruct students to write their comic strip as a story. The words in the dialogue balloons in the comic strip will be in quotations in the story.

Comic Strip Creation

Choose two characters and develop a storyline around them. Place characters' conversations in dialogue balloons in each cartoon frame.

1.

2.

3.

4.

5.

6.

WRITING DIRECTIONS

Materials:

• drawing paper
• lined paper
• pencils

Lesson Procedure

1. Ed Emberley relies completely on visual clues for his drawing instructions. Challenge students to add some written instructions that coincide with the step-by-step pictures.
2. Encourage each student to select a simple drawing from *Ed Emberley's Big Orange Drawing Book.*
3. Have students divide a sheet of drawing paper into as many boxes as there are steps in their chosen drawing.
4. Have students draw a sequential step in each box on their paper so the steps are replicated exactly as they appear in Ed Emberley's book.
5. Now, challenge students to write instructions for the step inside each box.

Taking It Further . . .

Challenge students to give a partner auditory clues for drawing a picture from *Ed Emberley's Big Orange Drawing Book.* Have partners sit back to back. One partner holds the book and describes how a drawing is made. The other partner draws the described picture.

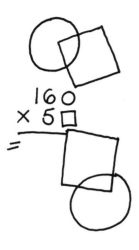

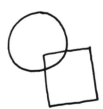

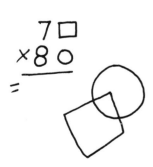

Materials:

•5" x 7" cards
•pencils
•crayons or markers

Lesson Procedure

1. Draw one of Ed Emberley's final products on the chalkboard. (Do not "fill in" the drawing as indicated in the final steps. When filled in, it is difficult to see the individual shapes that make up the complete drawing.)
2. Write several math questions and problems to solve based on the drawing.

   How many rectangles do you see?
   How many circles do you see?
   Multiply the number of rectangles by the number of circles.

3. Give each student a 5" x 7" card.
4. Invite each student to choose one of Ed Emberley's drawings and draw it on the card. Remind students not to "fill in" the drawings.
5. Underneath the drawings, encourage students to write math questions and problems.
6. Have students write the answers on the back of the cards to add a self-checking feature.
7. Make the cards available at a math center.

Taking It Further . . .

Make a class book of math problems. Bind the 5" x 7" cards with rings. Students will enjoy adding new pages.

# SCARY ANIMALS

Materials:

- •butcher paper (black and white)
- •construction paper (assorted colors)
- •lined paper
- •scissors
- •pencils
- •white crayon or chalk
- •crayons or markers
- •glue
- •encyclopedias

Lesson Procedure

1. Enlist the students' help to design a large haunted house for the bulletin board using the directions in *Ed Emberley's Big Orange Drawing Book.*
2. Use a white crayon or chalk to draw the house on black butcher paper.
3. Cut out the windows and back the openings with white butcher paper. Encourage the students to add scary details to the walls of the house.
4. Cut out letters to label the bulletin board "Who Is Scary?"
5. Encourage students to tell what wild animals they consider to be scary and why.
6. Help students understand the reasons behind some of the animal behaviors that appear frightening. For example, animals make fierce noises as a means of protection against their enemies.
7. Ask students or pairs of students to select a wild animal and tell why people often view it as frightening.
8. Invite students to write a report explaining the animal's behavior.
9. Have students make pictures of their animals and mount them in the windows of the haunted house.
10. Mount the reports around the outside of the house.

Taking It Further . .

Students will enjoy planning skits in which animals and humans talk about who is the most frightening and why.

Ed Emberley's

Especially appropriate for holidays, such as Valentine's Day and Christmas, this book is full of red-hot drawing ideas. The ambitious artist will enjoy the challenge of drawing Santa's sleigh and eight reindeer.

Boston: Little, Brown & Company, 1987

Big Red Drawing Book

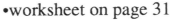
HOLIDAY GREETINGS

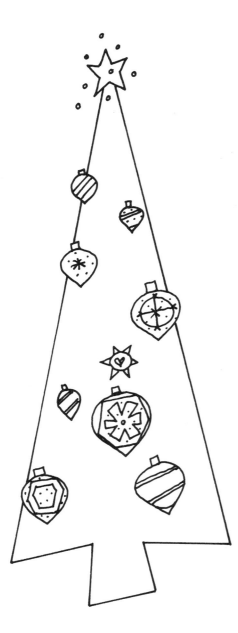

Materials:

- worksheet on page 31
- green construction or butcher paper
- pencils
- crayons, colored pencils, or markers

Lesson Procedure

1. Practice drawing some of the holiday designs from *Ed Emberley's Big Red Drawing Book* with the students.
2. Invite students to use their favorite holiday designs to decorate the ornament on the worksheet.
3. Encourage students to color the designs and cut out the completed ornaments.
4. Suggest that students write a holiday greeting to a friend or family member on the back of the ornaments.
5. Make a giant Christmas tree on a bulletin board. Hang all the decorated ornaments on the tree.
6. Invite family members to come and find their child's greeting.

Taking It Further . . .

As a book-evaluating activity, students can decorate an ornament as a character in a favorite book might decorate it. On the back of the ornament, students can write the title and author, as well as a brief opinion of the book.

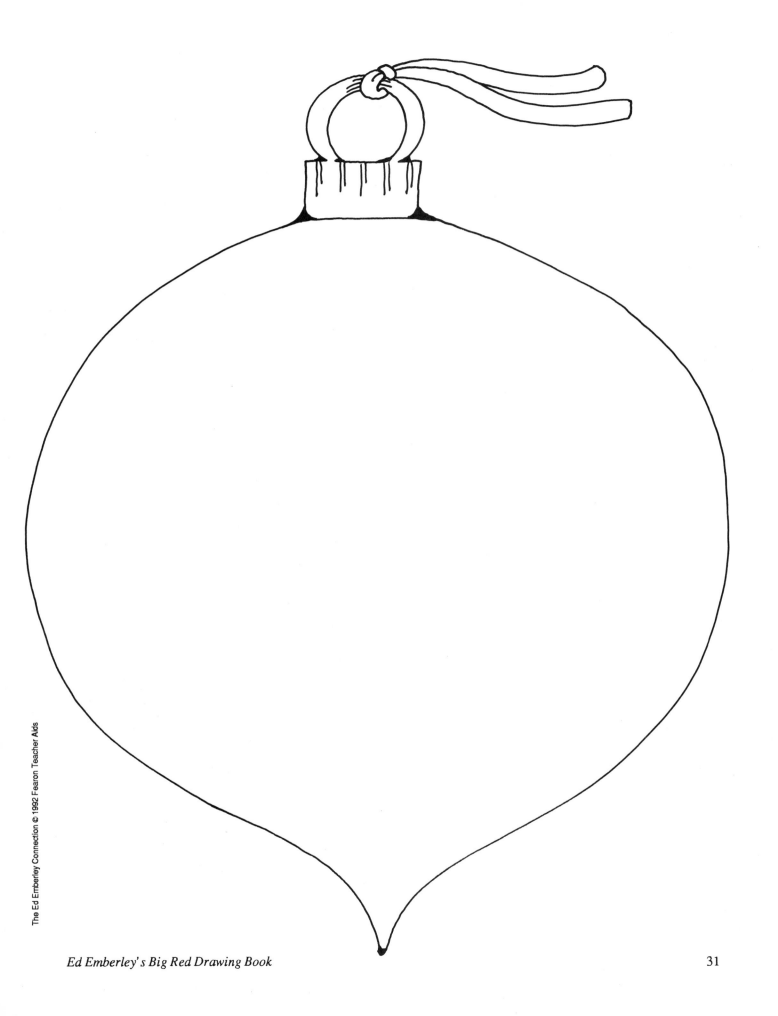

Ed Emberley's Big Red Drawing Book

✦ MINI-PICTURE DICTIONARY ✦

Materials:

- worksheet on page 33
- pencils
- crayons or markers

Lesson Procedure

1. Discuss how Ed Emberley connects simple lines to create pictures. Explain that students will be making their own mini-picture dictionaries using ideas from Ed Emberley's drawing books.
2. Give each student three copies of the worksheet.
3. Students can use the back of one of the pages as a title page for the dictionary by writing "Mini-Dictionary" and their name on that page.
4. Demonstrate how to do a page of entries. For each entry, write the uppercase letter in the box on the left side of the page, a word that begins with that letter on the line, and draw a picture of that word in the box on the right. There will be three entries on each small page.

5. Encourage students to complete an entry for each of the 26 letters of the alphabet.
6. Students can cut out each page and staple all the pages together to make a mini-booklet.

Taking It Further . . .

Use the mini-dictionaries as spelling lists, story starters, or oral-reading booklets. Mini-dictionaries are especially effective for second-language acquisition.

 · TRANSPORTATION ·

Materials:

- drawing paper
- lined paper
- construction paper (various colors)
- pencils
- crayons or markers
- encyclopedias and reference books

Lesson Procedure

1. Give each student the opportunity to select a ship or truck to draw from *Ed Emberley's Big Red Drawing Book.*
2. Invite each student to draw the ship or truck on a sheet of drawing paper.
3. Challenge students to use encyclopedias or reference books about transportation to research information about the ship or truck they drew. Information might include size, distinguishing characteristics, and purpose.
4. Have students write the facts on a sheet of lined paper.
5. Invite students to color their pictures and mount them on construction paper, along with their reports. Display the reports and illustrations on a transportation bulletin board

Taking It Further . . .

Make a transportation bulletin board promoting books about vehicles. Put up a background of black and gray skyscrapers, a blue river or bay, and red bridges. Ask students to cut out shapes of trucks and ships. On these shapes, invite students to write titles of books about transportation. Have the books available for independent reading on a table near the bulletin board.

Ed Emberley's

If you can draw six simple lines, you can create a variety of interesting faces using Ed Emberley's step-by-step guide. From Starlet Stella and Admiral Andrew all the way to Hairy Dog Henry, you'll be amazed how the lines begin to take shape.

Boston: Little, Brown & Company, 1975

Drawing Book of Faces

CREATING CHARACTER

Materials:

- drawing paper
- lined paper
- pencils

Lesson Procedure

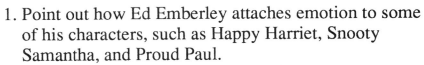

1. Point out how Ed Emberley attaches emotion to some of his characters, such as Happy Harriet, Snooty Samantha, and Proud Paul.
2. Invite students to choose their favorite face from the book and make a large drawing of it.
3. On lined paper, challenge students to list character attributes of the person behind the face they created. Students might also include a description of the character's physical appearance and unique mannerisms. Invite students to consider the following questions to stimulate thought about their character's description.

   How does your character move?
   How does your character talk?
   Does he/she have an accent or use special phrases?
   How does your character react to other people?

Taking It Further . . .

Encourage students to use their characters in a creative-writing lesson. Provide students an interesting setting in which to place their characters and then let their imaginations flow. The character may be stranded on an island, on a mission to outerspace, or deep-sea diving in the Atlantic Ocean.

MIXED-UP FACE GAME

Materials:

•drawing paper
•pencils

Lesson Procedure

1. Divide the class into groups of four. Have each student fold a piece of drawing paper into fourths lengthwise and then unfold the paper.
2. Invite each student to write his or her name in the top right-hand corner of the first section. In that same top section, have each student draw only the top of a person's head, forehead, and hair. (Be sure students extend the lines from the bottom of the head over the fold into the next section.)
3. Have students fold the top section back so it cannot be seen and pass the paper to their right.
4. When each student receives his or her neighbor's paper, they should write their name in the upper right-hand corner of the second section. Encourage students to draw the eyes, nose, and ears in this section, being sure to connect the outside lines to those from the forehead.
5. Have students fold this section back so it cannot be seen and again pass the paper to their right.
6. In the third section, each student should sign his or her name and draw a mouth and chin.
7. Have the students fold their section back and pass the paper to the right one last time.
8. In the fourth section, students should sign their name and draw a neck and shoulders to complete the drawing.
9. Students can open the papers to reveal the composite.

Taking It Further . . .

Students will enjoy experimenting with the book *Ed Emberley's Crazy Mixed-Up Face Game* (Boston: Little, Brown & Company, 1981).

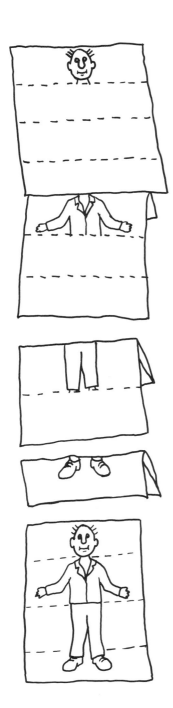

☙ • MIXED-UP BODY GAME • ❧

Materials:

• drawing paper
• pencils

Lesson Procedure

1. Follow the procedure for drawing, folding, and passing described in the "Mixed-Up Face Game" on page 37. However, in this activity, students will be drawing an entire body rather than just a head.
2. In the top section, students draw a head, extending the neck over the fold onto the next section.
3. In the second section, students draw an upper torso (from the waist up), arms, and hands, including shirt or top of dress. (Be sure the bottom lines of the torso extend over the fold onto the next section.)
4. In the third section, students draw the lower torso, legs, and ankles, including skirt or pants. Remind the students one last time to extend the lines of the ankles just below the fold.
5. In the last section, students draw feet and shoes.
6. Have students open the papers to reveal the composite.

Taking It Further . . .

Challenge each student to choose one composite picture and write a story about it. Display the pictures and stories on a bulletin board.

Ed Emberley's

Ed Emberley shows how to
add just a few lines to thumbprints
to create everything from football
players to singing pigs. After
adding a few more lines to create
movement and variations, these
critters definitely rate "two
thumbs up."

Boston: Little, Brown &
Company, 1977

Great
Thumbprint
Drawing Book

☙ • WRITING THUMBTHING • ❧

Materials:

- •worksheet on page 41
- •pencils
- •ink pad

Lesson Procedure

1. Challenge students to transform their thumbprints into pictures.
2. Have students press their thumbs on an ink pad and place their prints inside the boxes. Students can then draw creatures using their own thumbprints.
3. On the lines next to each thumbprint, students can write sentences or rhyming couplets.

I'm sending some mail,
To my friend, the whale.

Taking It Further . . .

Encourage students to use thumbprints to illustrate animal reports.

Writing Thumbthing

Turn your thumbprints into a picture by adding some details with your pencil. Then write a sentence or rhyming couplet to describe each picture.

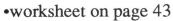

• WRITING PUNS •

Materials:

- worksheet on page 43
- lined paper
- transparency film
- ink pads
- paper towels
- pencils

Lesson Procedure

1. Make an overhead transparency of the worksheet on page 43.
2. Explain to students that a pun is a play on words. For example, I wanted a peanut butter *sand witch*, but she flew away.
3. Challenge students to suggest the puns pictured on the worksheet.

   1. thum**bing**bird
   2. national an**thumb**
   3. ele**thumb**

   4. opo**thumb**
   5. py**thumb**
   6. **thumb**erparty

4. In brainstorming groups of 3-4 students, challenge students to think of puns using "thumb." Invite students to write and illustrate their puns on lined paper. Use ink pads to make thumbprint pictures.

Taking It Further . . .

Students will enjoy finding additional puns in Ed Emberley's Thumbprint boxed set, including *Bugs and Beasts* and *Thumbpuns* (Boston: Little, Brown & Company, 1992).

1. _____

2. _____

3. _____

4. _____

5. _____

6. _____

WHO AM I?

Materials:

- •lined paper
- •ink pads
- •paper towels
- •soap and water
- •pencils

Lesson Procedure

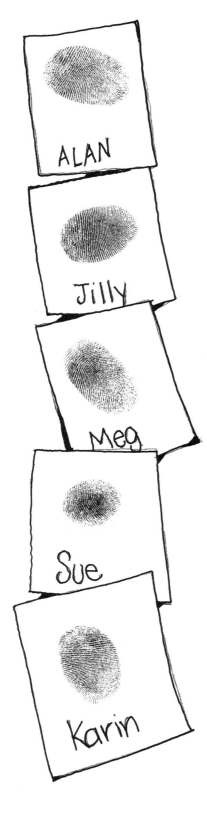

1. Discuss how everyone's thumbprint is unique.
2. On lined paper, have students make thumbprints using ink pads. (Provide soap, water, and paper towels to clean up afterwards.)
3. Invite students to title their papers "Who Am I?"
4. Ask students to provide statistical information about themselves.

birthdate	height	weight
hair color	eye color	national origin

5. Ask students to share additional information about themselves describing ways they are unique.

hobbies	interests	talents

6. Display the thumbprint reports on a bulletin board. Cover up each student's name and challenge classmates to guess who each thumbprint belongs to.

Taking It Further . . .

For a fun science activity, have students make their thumbprints on 3" x 5" cards. In groups of 6-8, invite students to analyze the different kinds of thumbprints using magnifying glasses (whorl, arch, and so on) and group them by similarities.

Ed Emberley's Great Thumbprint Drawing Book

Ed Emberley's

With creative flair and a dash of color, Ed Emberley shows how to create a variety of pictures using a circle that has been divided like a pie. There's no limit to the combination of fractional parts.

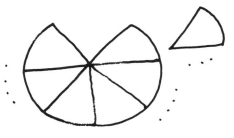

Boston: Little, Brown & Company, 1984

Picture Pie: A Circle Drawing Book

PIECING THE PICTURE

Materials:

- 9" x 12" construction paper (assorted colors)
- pencils
- compasses, paper cups, or coffee can lids
- scissors
- glue
- crayons or markers

Lesson Procedure

1. Discuss different ways Ed Emberley puts circles and circle parts together in his book to create pictures.
2. Invite students to select three or four colors of construction paper.
3. Have students trace circles using a compass, cup, or lid on all but one piece of paper.
4. Have students cut out all the circles. Suggest that students cut some circles into halves and some into fourths.
5. Encourage students to experiment with their shapes by placing different arrangements on the 9" x 12" paper they did not cut.
6. When students have decided on a pattern or picture they like, have them glue the pieces onto the paper.

Taking It Further . . .

After the pictures have dried completely, students can make crayon rubbings of the designs. Have students place a piece of white drawing paper over the tops of their collages and rub with the side of a crayon.

PIE GRAPHS

Materials:

- worksheet on page 48
- lined paper
- pencils
- crayons or markers

Lesson Procedure

1. Point out how all of Ed Emberley's pictures in *Ed Emberley's Picture Pie* are made from circles or parts of circles (fractions). These fractional parts are made by cutting the circles in half and then cutting the halves in half and so on.
2. In groups of 3-4, encourage students to select a topic of interest and take an opinion poll of the class. Topics might include favorite food, favorite TV show, family size, or eye color.
3. Instruct each polling group to divide their topic into four choices. For example, if students choose the topic of favorite food, their selections might include pizza, hamburger, spaghetti, and egg rolls.
4. When students poll the class, emphasize that they poll a number of students equal to a multiple of four (8, 12, 16).
5. Help students convert their data into approximate fractions. Note – All fractions may not work out evenly. Teacher may need to assist students in filling in the pie graphs.

   pizza $5/12 = 1/2$ hamburger $4/12 = 1/3$ spaghetti $2/12 = 1/6$ egg rolls $1/12 = 1/12$

6. Encourage students to label and color their pie-graph worksheets to show the results of their polls.

Taking It Further . . .

To simplify the fractional activity for younger students, give each child a worksheet divided into sixteenths. Invite each student to poll sixteen classmates. Have students color one section for each student polled. Remind students to use a different color for each of the four choices. Try to keep all the same colored squares together. Have the students count the number of squares for each color.

Pie Graph

Record the results of your poll by coloring in pieces of the circle. Use one color to represent each of your four choices. Label what each color represents and what fractional part of the whole it is.

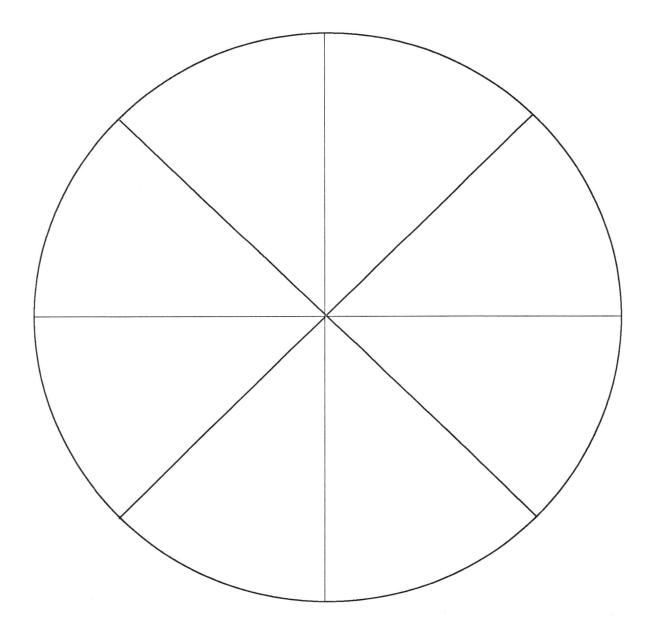

The Ed Emberley Connection © 1992 Fearon Teacher Aids

Ed Emberley's Picture Pie

☙ PIE PLATE ANIMAL QUIZ ☙

Materials:

- 9" paper plates
- 9" x 12" construction paper (assorted colors)
- 12" rulers, dowels, or cardboard strips
- paper cups
- pencils
- scissors
- glue
- masking tape

Lesson Procedure

1. Discuss some of the animals Ed Emberley created in his book using circles and parts of circles.
2. Invite students to select several colors of construction paper and trace circles using paper cups.
3. Have students cut out their circles, cutting some of them into smaller fractional pieces ($1/2$, $1/4$, $1/8$). Encourage students to arrange the pieces on a paper plate to create an animal. Have students glue the pieces in place.
4. On the back of the paper plate, instruct each student to write a riddle about his or her animal that ends with the question, "Who am I?"
5. Have students tape their paper plates to a ruler, dowel, or cardboard strip for a handle.
6. Students can take turns sharing their riddles with the class.

Taking It Further . . .

Give students another paper plate. Have students draw lines dividing their plates into fourths. On one fourth, invite students to write an introduction to their animal that begins with an intriguing fact. On the next two fourths, tell where their animal lives, what it eats, and some interesting behavioral facts. Students can use the last fourth to record the most interesting fact about their animal.

• PEOPLE PIE •

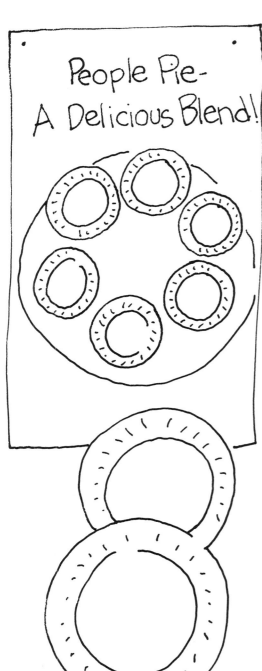

Materials:

- small paper plates
- crayons or markers
- pencils

Lesson Procedure

1. Explain that just as each piece of a circle is part of the whole, so each individual is an important part of an entire community.
2. Invite each student to view him or herself as an important part of your classroom community. Encourage students to think of ways they may be different from their classmates (culture, physical attributes, personality characteristics, accomplishments, family customs and traditions, talents).
3. Discuss the important contributions made by each student as a result of his or her uniqueness.
4. Have students draw a picture of their contribution to the classroom on a paper plate.
5. Make a large pie on a bulletin board and mount each individual paper plate within the circle. The bulletin board can be titled "People Pie—A Delicious Blend!"

Taking It Further . . .

Extend the activity by asking students to research contributions made by members of their community.

Bits and Bytes—

For those who cannot tell a "mouse" from a "ram" and want to give their computer a "boot," this little book is a good beginning. With it, students can learn the meanings of the most commonly used computer terms and keep the "bugs" away from their "turtles."

Written by Seymour Simon
Illustrated by Barbara and
Ed Emberley
New York: Thomas Y. Crowell,
1985

A Computer Dictionary for Beginners

ASCII ME ANYTHING

Materials:

•lined paper
•pencils

Lesson Procedure

1. Review and discuss the computer terms *bits* and *bytes*.

   A *bit* is one piece of information.
   A *byte* (eight bits) is a computer code that stands for a letter, number, or symbol.

2. Explain ASCII to the children—the base-ten system that we use to understand the computer's binary (base-two) system. ASCII assigns a number to every symbol.
3. Write the ASCII code on the chalkboard.

A	= 65	H	= 72	O	= 79	V	= 86
B	= 66	I	= 73	P	= 80	W	= 87
C	= 67	J	= 74	Q	= 81	X	= 88
D	= 68	K	= 75	R	= 82	Y	= 89
E	= 69	L	= 76	S	= 83	Z	= 90
F	= 70	M	= 77	T	= 84		
G	= 71	N	= 78	U	= 85		

4. Give each student a sheet of lined paper. Challenge students to write questions and answers to one another in ASCII.

   72-79-87   65-82-69   89-79-85
   (H O W   A R E   Y O U?)

   73   65-77   70-73-78-69
   (I   A M   F I N E.)

Taking It Further . . .

Before the students arrive in the morning, write a message on the chalkboard in ASCII. The message might tell students whose turn it is to work on the computer or whose turn it is to read a book.

Materials:

•1/2" grid paper
•pencils

Lesson Procedure

1. Review the definition of "Logo" in *Bits and Bytes*—a computer program that lets you draw pictures on the screen with a "turtle." If students are familiar with the program, this activity can be used as extended practice during "off computer" times. If students do not have access to a computer or this program, the exercise is a great listening activity.

2. The step-by step directions include information that is necessary for the program "Logo." If your students are not familiar with this program, disregard the 90° notation when explaining the directions to the class. Instruct the students to turn their papers (quarter turn) to the right or the left as directed, so they are always facing the same direction as the line they have just drawn.

3. Give each student a sheet of grid paper and dictate the following directions.

1. Place your paper horizontally on your desk.
2. Locate the bottom left-hand corner.
3. Count four full spaces to the right and four full spaces up. Each 1/2" square is considered a full space.
4. Draw an "X" where the two lines intersect. This is your starting place. (Challenge students to draw only on the grid lines and to not lift their pencils from their papers.)
5. Move forward 1.
6. Move right (90°), then forward 1.
7. Move left (90°), then forward 1.
8. Move right (90°), then forward 1.
9. Move left (90°), then forward 1.
10. Move right (90°), then forward 2.
11. Move left (90°), then forward 1.
12. Move right (90°), then forward 2.
13. Move right (90°), then forward 1.
14. Move left (90°), then forward 2.
15. Move right (90°), then forward 1.
16. Move left (90°), then forward 1.
17. Move right (90°), then forward 1.
18. Move left (90°), then forward 1.
19. Move left (90°), then forward 1.
20. Move right (90°), then forward 2.
21. Move right (90°), then forward 2.
22. Move right (90°), then forward 4.
23. Move left (90°), then forward 1.
24. Move right (90°), then forward 2.
25. Move right (90°), then forward 1.
26. Move left (90°), then forward 2.
27. Move left (90°), then forward 1.
28. Move right (90°), then forward 2.
29. Move right (90°), then forward 1.
30. Move left (90°), then forward 2.

4. As an alternative activity, invite students to draw the turtle using "Logo" on their computers (if available). Follow the same directions, but change all forward commands to multiples of ten. For example, "forward 1" would become "forward 10."

Taking It Further . . .

For further practice, see *Grid and Bear It* and *Grid and Graph It*, two books by Will C. Howell (Carthage, IL: Fearon Teacher Aids, 1987).

How to Talk

An easy introduction to computer communication, this book shows that talking to a computer is easy if you know the language. Unlike people, computers cannot think for themselves and so directions must be specific and orderly.

HEY THERE

Written by Seymour Simon
Illustrated by Barbara and
Ed Emberley
New York: Thomas Y. Crowell,
1985

to Your Computer

TURTLE WALK

Materials:

•14" x 22" tagboard

Lesson Procedure

1. Ask students if they remember the name of the computer language used for drawing lines and pictures ("Logo"). Students can practice giving commands in "Logo" for this activity.
2. Have students sit in a square formation on the floor. Explain that they represent the top, sides, and bottom of a computer monitor.
3. Select one student to be the "turtle." Cut a point at one end of a piece of tagboard to make an arrow. Cut a 9" hole in the center of the arrow and place over the "turtle's" head.
4. Explain to the students that in the program "Logo" the directions include 90° turns (quarter turns) either right or left and the number of steps to take. Demonstrate for the students how to follow the "Logo" instructions.
5. Then place the turtle in the "home" position in the center of the "screen."
6. Students can take turns giving the "turtle" "Logo" directions.

   turn left 90°   turn right 90°
   move forward 2 steps   move forward 4 steps

7. The object is to keep the "turtle" moving without running into the edges of the "screen."

Taking It Further . . .

Place four chairs in the center of the "screen." Challenge students to take turns giving the "turtle" "Logo" directions to guide him or her around the chairs and back "home."

WRITING NON-FICTION

Materials:

- worksheet on page 58
- lined paper
- pencils
- reference books
- file cards

Lesson Procedure

1. Point out how Seymour Simon and Ed Emberley have chosen a topic of interest to them (computers) and written a non-fiction book about it. Non-fiction is an important book category. Some non-fiction authors children may enjoy include Jean Fritz, Ruth Heller, Patricia Lauber, and Russell Freedman.
2. Suggest some non-fiction topics for writing projects and help the students make a selection.

   animals   computers   biographies   countries
   machines   sports

3. Suggest that students research and record each fact they discover about their topics on a separate file card.
4. Invite students to organize their facts into three main areas and record the subtopics on the worksheet provided on page 58. Remind students that they will probably not be able to use all of the information they have gathered.
5. Instruct students to organize their fact cards in a logical sequence and write the appropriate facts under each subtopic heading.
6. Encourage students to use the information on their worksheets to write a paragraph for each subtopic on lined paper.

Taking It Further . . .

Encourage students to use their worksheets and paragraphs to organize a picturebook complete with illustrations.

Name _____

Non-Fiction Writing

Topic _____

I. _____
   (subtopic)

   A. _____

   B. _____

   C. _____

II. _____
    (subtopic)

   A. _____

   B. _____

   C. _____

III. _____
     (subtopic)

   A. _____

   B. _____

   C. _____

The Ed Emberley Connection © 1992 Fearon Teacher Aids

Klippity Klop

The story follows the format of the well-known children's chant about going on a bear hunt. But this hunt takes place in medieval times. The soft, black line drawings on brown pages create a book that is visually intriguing.

Boston: Little, Brown & Company, 1974

Materials:

- 12" x 18" green construction paper
- pencils
- pinking shears
- crayons or markers

Lesson Procedure

1. Cut construction paper into 4" x 18" strips.
2. Give one green construction-paper strip to each student.
3. Have students fold their strips in half twice, unfold the strips, and then refold accordion style.

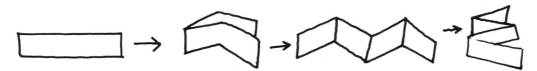

4. Across the top of the paper, have students draw a curved line. Using pinking shears, cut on the curved line to create a textured dragon back.
5. Have the students decide where the head and tail should be located. Invite students to draw a capital letter "B" for eyes and another capital "B" for a nose. Encourage students to add a snout, teeth, a tail, and a front foot.

6. On the inside of their dragon booklets, students can write appropriate stories.

Taking It Further . . .

Invite students to think of other ways to use their dragon books, such as recording difficult spelling "dragons."

WORDLESS BOOK

Materials:

- worksheets on pages 63-64
- drawing paper
- pencils
- scissors
- stapler

Lesson Procedure

1. Reproduce the two worksheets back-to-back, with page 2 appearing directly behind the title page.
2. Give each student a double-sided worksheet and have students write their names on the title pages.
3. Many books are printed in sheets of 16 or 32 pages. These press sheets are then folded to form a book or a section of a book. Each folded sheet is known as a signature. Explain to students that they will be creating miniature books using miniature signatures.
4. Ask students to recall the events of the story in the order in which they happened.

   Prince Krispin and Dumpling go for a ride (page 2).
   They ride over a bridge (page 3).
   They cross a stream (page 4).
   They ride through a field (page 5).
   They ride down a gravelly hill (page 6).
   They ride up a rocky hill (page 7).
   They look in a cave and see a dragon (page 8).

5. Invite students to draw a picture of each of the seven events on the pages of their booklets.
6. Have students fold the completed worksheets into fourths so the title page is in the front. Staple the spine and trim the folded edges across the top.
7. Students can retell the story of Prince Krispin and Dumpling using their wordless picturebooks. When they reach the end, they can "read" the story backwards to retrace the journey back to the castle.

Taking It Further . . .

Discuss the cyclical nature of the story *Klippity Klop*. Encourage students to write new stories using a circular theme.

Illustrated by _____

by Ed Emberley

Klippity Klop

5

4

7

2

6

3

Klippity Klop

The Ed Emberley Connection © 1992 Fearon Teacher Aids

 SOUND SYMPHONY

Materials:

Lesson Procedure

1. Read the story again and encourage students to read the sound-effect words with you.
2. Encourage students to brainstorm ways the sound effects for each scene could be made in the classroom.

   klippity-klop (tapping fingertips on desk)
   bridge (rub open palms on desk)
   stream (make slurping noise)
   field (rub palms on legs)
   gravelly hill (tapping fingernails on desk)
   rocky hill (tapping knuckles on desk)
   castle door (loud clap)

3. Reread the story and invite students to make the sound effects at the appropriate time.

Taking It Further . . .

Provide students with other books that could have sound effects added, such as *Parade* by Donald Crews (New York: Greenwillow Books, 1983), *Wheel Away!* by Dayle Ann Dodds (New York: Harper & Row, 1989), or *The Wheels on the Bus* by Maryann Kovalski (Boston: Joy Street Books, 1989). Invite students to compose sound effects for the stories and present them to the class.

❧ • RAPUNZEL SLEPT HERE • ❧

Materials:

- worksheet on page 67
- fairy tales
- pencils

Lesson Procedure

1. Remind students that Prince Krispin and Dumpling found a dragon living in the castle. Discuss other fairy-tale characters who also lived in a castle.

Rapunzel	Prince Charming
Sleeping Beauty	Wicked Queen from Snow White

2. Invite students to use the worksheet on page 67 to describe the castle setting from a fairy-tale character's point of view. For example, Rapunzel's description might begin like this:

   "Do you think it is all roses sleeping in a castle? That would depend on who you are. I live in a damp, cold stone tower. There's nothing covering the windows and it gets really cold at night . . . ."

3. After students have written their stories, ask them to share their ideas with the class.

Taking It Further . . .

Make a game out of the story sharing by having students withhold the identity of their characters as they read. Encourage the class to guess who the character might be and from which fairy tale.

Klippity Klop

Name _____

_____ **Slept Here**

Klippity Klop

STORY MAPPING

Materials:

- drawing paper
- pencils
- crayons, colored pencils, or markers

Lesson Procedure

1. Make a list of the places Prince Krispin and Dumpling went on their ride.

bridge	stream	field
gravelly hill	rocky hill	cave
castle		

2. Individually or in small cooperative groups, students can map out Prince Krispin's route on drawing paper.
3. Remind students to show the entire round-trip journey.
4. Students can also add a map key, mileage scale, and color the map as well.

Taking It Further . . .

Students can draw the map on 1/2" grid paper to make a game. Taking turns, students move their markers the number of grid squares indicated by the roll of the dice. The player who first completes the round trip is the winner.

Klippity Klop

DRAGON MATH

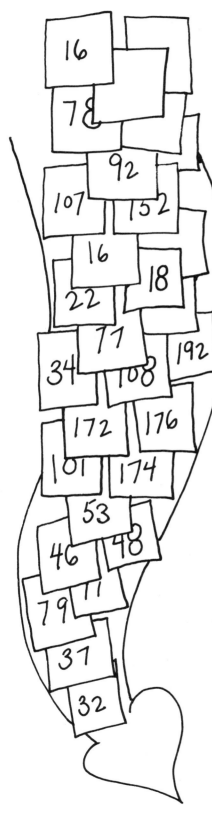

Materials:

- worksheet on page 70
- green construction paper
- pencils
- glue

Lesson Procedure

1. Make one copy of the worksheet provided on page 70. Fill in each of the twenty-five squares with an appropriate math problem. Make a copy of the worksheet for each student.
2. Cut the green construction paper in squares just slightly larger than 1" x 1" and give each student twenty-five pieces.
3. Invite students to write the answers to the math problems on the green squares and then glue each square onto the worksheet on top of the correct math problem. Students should start gluing at the bottom of the page so the green dragon scales overlap from the top down.

Taking It Further . . .

Using an opaque projector, copy the dragon worksheet on a 3' x 4' piece of butcher paper. Make four giant dragons and write math problems in each square. Divide the class into four teams. Have a contest to see which team can correctly complete the problems first.

The Ed Emberley Connection © 1992 Fearon Teacher Aids

 DRAGONS I'VE FOUGHT

Materials:

- worksheet on page 72
- pencils

Lesson Procedure

1. Discuss the encounter with the dragon in *Klippity Klop* and how Prince Krispin chose to deal with the problem (retreat).
2. Ask students to make a list of ways they have dealt with problems of their own. Ideas may include fighting back, reasoning, or ignoring the situation.
3. Discuss problems students might face at home or at school. Ideas may include being unfairly punished, having something that belongs to you destroyed or taken away, or being unable to spend time with a family member or good friend.
4. Invite students to use the worksheet on page 72 to list some problems they have encountered.
5. Students can think of ways to deal with the problems and write the solution possibilities on the lines around each dragon.
6. Encourage students to share, with the class, a problem they have encountered and how they dealt with it. Sharing will help students realize that they are not alone in the problems that they face. It will also help them consider new solutions.

Taking It Further . . .

Select several common problems and write them on large paper dragons. Mount the dragons on a bulletin board. Provide blank cards for students to suggest solutions. Mount the solutions around the appropriate dragons.

Dragons I've Fought

In each dragon, write a problem you have encountered. Around each dragon, list some ways you could deal with the problems.

The Ed Emberley Connection © 1992 Fearon Teacher Aids

Klippity Klop

CREATING A DRAGON

Materials:

- drawing paper
- construction paper, tissue paper, and foil (assorted colors)
- gift wrap scraps
- wallpaper samples
- magazines and newspapers
- pencils
- scissors
- glue

Lesson Procedure

1. Ask students to describe the dragon in *Klippity Klop*. Invite volunteers to draw their own versions of what a dragon might look like on the chalkboard.
2. Encourage each student to draw a large dragon on a piece of white drawing paper.
3. Invite students to cut 1" square "scales" from the colored paper scraps and wallpaper samples.
4. Have students glue the scales to their dragons. Be sure students start gluing at the bottom of the dragons and work their way up so the scales will overlap. Emphasize texture and pattern.

Taking It Further . . .

Students can experiment creating textured dragon scales using clay, wood, wire, or fabric.

⮜• GROCERY BAG HELMETS •⮞

Materials:

- •large grocery bags
- •pencils
- •scissors
- •crayons or markers

Lesson Procedure

1. Give each student a grocery bag.
2. Demonstrate how students might design a helmet for Prince Krispin. Then encourage students to decorate helmets of their own.

Helmet 1

1. Cut out a large hole in the front of the bag for the face.
2. Draw a line straight down from the face hole. Add small circles next to the line for rivets.

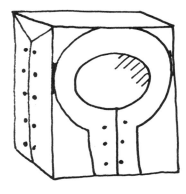

Helmet 2

1. Draw a large "V" at the top of the bag.
2. Cut several rectangular slits in the "V" for students to see through.
3. Cut a slit under the "V" for the mouth.

Taking It Further . . .

Younger students will enjoy having a Knight Parade wearing their helmets as they march through the school.

MY HOME IS MY CASTLE

Materials:

•worksheet on page 76
•pencils

Lesson Procedure

1. Discuss the phrase, "A person's home is his or her castle." Ask students what they think the saying means. What makes a home a castle? What made Prince Krispin's castle a home?
2. At the top of the worksheet on page 76, students can draw their homes as they look now.
3. On the bottom of the worksheet, invite students to draw their homes with features they would like to add to make their dream homes a "castle."

Taking It Further . . .

Instead of drawing, suggest that students write about their homes. Ask students to describe their homes as they look now and then consider ways to make them better. (Be sensitive to each child's individual living situation.) Encourage students to consider possibilities other than physical changes as well.

Name _____

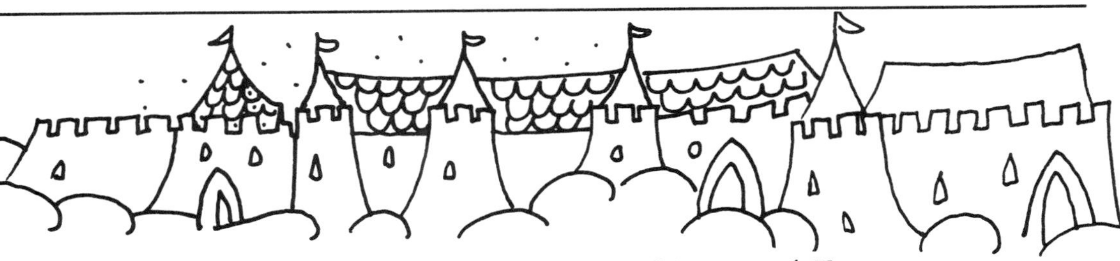

My Home Is My Castle

Before

After

The Ed Emberley Connection © 1992 Fearon Teacher Aids

Klippity Klop

One Wide River

Using bright and animated woodcuts, Ed Emberley illustrates this charming old folk song of Noah and the great flood. From shoeless alligators to skating snakes, the animals file in the ark to cross the wide river.

Adapted by Barbara Emberley
Englewood Cliffs, NJ: Prentice-Hall, 1966

to Cross

❧ • WRITING COUPLETS • ❧

Materials:

•worksheet on page 79
•pencils

Lesson Procedure

1. Reread each pair of rhyming sentences throughout the story, leaving out the final words. Encourage students to supply the missing rhymes.

   "The animals came in four by four.
   The hippopotamus blocked the _____ ."

2. Give each student a copy of the worksheet on page 79.
3. Invite students to compose original rhyming second lines.
4. Students may enjoy brainstorming ideas in pairs or small groups.

Taking It Further . . .

Using the new versions of rhyming couplets, invite students to illustrate the verses on long strips of adding-machine tape.

One Wide River to Cross

Write the second line for each rhyming couplet.

The animals came in one by one,

_____.

The animals came in two by two,

_____.

The animals came in three by three,

_____.

The animals came in four by four,

_____.

The animals came in five by five,

_____.

The animals came in six by six,

_____.

The animals came in seven by seven,

_____.

The animals came in eight by eight,

_____.

The animals came in nine by nine,

_____.

The animals came in ten by ten,

_____.

❧• READING ARK •❧

Materials:

- construction paper
- butcher paper
- pencils
- crayons or markers
- scissors
- straight pins or stapler

Lesson Procedure

1. Using butcher paper, make a large ark for the bulletin board. Label the bulletin board "The Reading Ark."
2. Explain to the class that they will be keeping track of all of the books that they read that are about animals.
3. Each time the students read a fiction or non-fiction book about animals, invite them to cut an animal shape from construction paper.
4. On the animal shape, write the book title, the author, and the illustrator. If space allows, encourage students to write a comment or two about the book as well.
5. Invite students to pin or staple the animals to the ark. The "Reading Ark" will hopefully motivate students to read even more books.

Taking It Further . . .

Use the information from the "Reading Ark" to make a game of titles, authors, and illustrators. On 3" x 5" cards, write questions, such as "Who wrote a book about a bear?" "What animal can be found in Tomie DePaola's *Bill and Pete*?" or "Who won a Caldecott award for drawing ducks?"

STORYBOARDS

Materials:

•worksheet on page 82
•pencils

Lesson Procedure

1. Discuss the important elements of a picturebook. Aliki's *How a Book Is Made* (New York: Thomas Y. Crowell, 1986) is helpful in providing background information about designing and publishing books. For additional information, you might want to use Uri Shulevitz' *Writing with Pictures* (New York: Watson-Guptill, 1985).

   Many picture books have 32 pages.
   Page 1 is often the title page.
   The copyright page often follows the title page, but can also be
   at the end of the book.
   Facing pages should look good side-by-side.

2. Invite students to use the worksheet on page 82 to make a storyboard of a favorite picturebook. Have students make a small thumbnail sketch of what is on each page.
3. Give students another worksheet to make a storyboard of their own original story. Younger students may find it easier to work with sixteen pages or even eight. Rather than use the worksheet, fold a piece of drawing paper in half three times to make eight boxes or four times to make sixteen.
4. Help students edit and revise their ideas to create a story with a good beginning, smooth flow through the middle, and a strong ending.
5. Encourage students to share their storyboards with one another.

Taking It Further . . .

Invite students to use their storyboards to develop a picturebook. Help them plan paper size, art media, and cover design.

Name _____

Storyboard

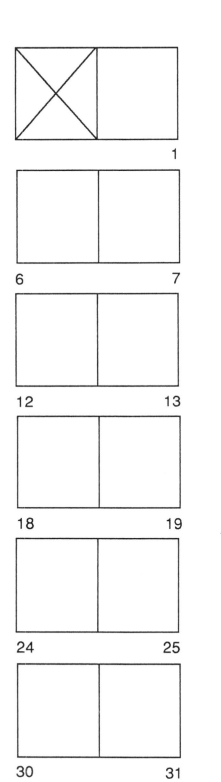

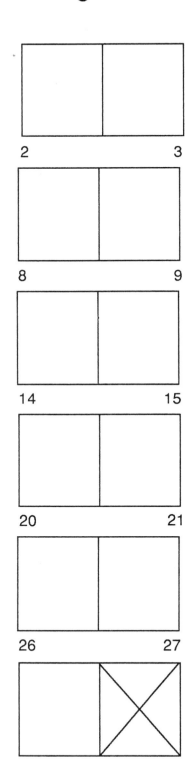

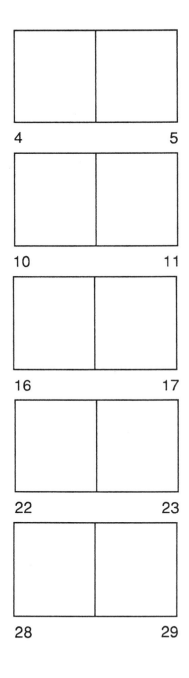

The Ed Emberley Connection © 1992 Fearon Teacher Aids

One Wide River to Cross

🐦 THE SYNONYMS ARE COMING 🐦

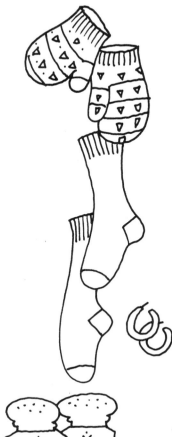

Materials:

- worksheet on page 84
- thesaurus
- pencils

Lesson Procedure

1. Remind students that some animals came "two by two" in Ed Emberley's story.
2. Ask students to brainstorm other objects that come in pairs (mittens, shoes, socks).
3. Encourage students to think of word pairs that have similar meanings (synonyms).

   cap—hat   smell—odor   party—celebration

4. Have students use the worksheet provided on page 84 to list several synonyms. Suggest that some students write only verb synonyms and others write only adjective synonyms to add variety to the end results.
5. Encourage students to use a thesaurus to extend their vocabulary.
6. Use the student lists to compile a larger list for a class bulletin board. Students can use the bulletin board as a resource when writing stories.

Taking It Further . . .

To encourage students to stretch their vocabulary, make a copy of the worksheet and fill one blank of each pair with a word students commonly use. Duplicate the worksheet and challenge students to think of interesting synonyms for these often over-used words.

Name _____

The Synonyms Are Coming Two by Two

1. _____
2. _____

1. _____
2. _____

1. _____
2. _____

1. _____
2. _____

1. _____
2. _____

1. _____
2. _____

1. _____
2. _____

1. _____
2. _____

1. _____
2. _____

The Ed Emberley Connection © 1992 Fearon Teacher Aids

☙• POSTCARDS FROM THE ARK •☙

Materials:

- 3" x 5" cards
- pencils

Lesson Procedure

1. List the animals that were on the ark as mentioned in the story and encourage students to think of others that might have been on the journey as well.
2. Discuss how the animals on the ark might have felt about the experience.

   Crocodiles would miss basking on a muddy shore.
   Giraffes would resent hitting their heads on the rafters.
   Kangaroos would have to be rescued when they jumped a bit too far over the edge of the ark.

3. Hand out a 3" x 5" card to each student. Invite students to choose one animal and write a postcard message from that animal's point of view. Suggest some opening lines to get students started.

   Wish you were here!
   There is never a dull moment on the ark.
   Noah isn't fair.

4. Invite students to read their postcards to the class.

Taking It Further . . .

Encourage students to include problems, concerns, or ideas that relate specifically to the animal they have chosen as they write a postcard message. When they read the postcard aloud to the class, encourage others to guess what animal would have written such a message.

COME ABOARD

Materials:

Lesson Procedure

1. Ask the students to sit in a circle for this pattern game.
2. Explain that you have a secret rule for entering the ark. Each student must suggest a word they think will fit the rule. If the word qualifies, the student may "come aboard." If the word does not fit the secret rule, the student must "stay ashore."
3. Begin with a rule, such as "You must bring a word with a double letter." Do not tell the students the rule, but give them some examples of words that qualify and examples of those that would not.

   alligator, but not crocodile   buffalo, but not bison   cookie, but not cake

4. The game can be ended whenever the leader chooses to reveal the rule. Students may enjoy continuing the game throughout the week until everyone has figured out the rule. In this case, it is helpful to keep a chart of qualifying words to help students see the pattern.
5. Try the game using different rules.

   words with two syllables
   collective nouns
   male/female animal pairs, such as *buck* and *doe*
   foods that go together, such as *bread* and *butter*

Taking It Further . . .

Write a qualifying word on the chalkboard each morning as students arrive. As students suggest other words that might fit the secret rule, write those that qualify on the chalkboard. Write the student's name beside the word. Students with qualifying words can be given special privileges for the day.

THE JORDAN TIMES

Materials:

- •worksheet on page 88
- •crayons or markers
- •scissors
- •laminator or clear adhesive paper

Lesson Procedure

1. Duplicate two worksheets to make a set of twenty-two cards for each group of four students.
2. Have students color the worksheets. Laminate the colored worksheets or cover with clear adhesive paper and cut the cards apart.
3. Before playing the game, review how the animals in *One Wide River to Cross* came into the ark one by one, two by two, three by three, and so on up to ten.
4. Divide the class into groups of four students. Each group begins the game by placing a deck of twenty-two cards face down between them.
5. Students take turns turning over one card at a time. In the first round, students multiply the revealed number by one. In the second round, students multiply the revealed number by two. Rounds continue to ten.
6. Students who multiply correctly keep the card. Students who multiply incorrectly put the card back in the deck. Each round continues until all the cards have been won.
7. The student with the most cards wins the game.
8. Younger students can play by adding the appropriate number to each revealed card rather than multiplying.

Taking It Further . . .

Vary the game by having two players sit opposite one another, each with a deck of twenty-two cards in front of them. Both players turn over a card at the same time. The first player to call out the correct product (or sum) wins the two cards. (To keep the decks separate, mark the back of each card in a deck with a symbol. Use a different symbol for each deck.)

4	8	**Jordan Times**
3	7	0 zero
2	6	10
1	5	9

One Wide River to Cross

ANIMAL REPORTS

Materials:

- worksheet on page 90
- brown butcher paper
- lined paper
- drawing paper
- pencils
- crayons, colored pencils, or markers
- reference books

Lesson Procedure

1. Draw a large ark on brown butcher paper, cut it out, and mount it on a bulletin board.
2. Invite students to select an animal to research and report on.
3. Instruct students to provide information for each question on the worksheet. Advanced students may wish to add a sheet of lined paper and provide additional information on how the animal relates to humans and whether it is endangered or not and why.
4. After organizing and editing their facts, encourage students to write their reports on lined paper.
5. Encourage students to draw pictures of their animals on drawing paper.
6. Mount the reports and pictures on the ark.

Taking It Further . . .

Invite students to turn their animal reports into booklets. Have each student make a cover the shape of their animal and cut pages to fit. Challenge students to include illustrations, maps, and diagrams.

Animal Report on

_____

A. Shelter

1. In what part of the world does the animal live?

_____

_____

2. In what kind of environment does the animal live?

_____

_____

B. Food

1. What does the animal eat? _____

_____

2. How does it acquire its food? _____

_____

C. Appearance

1. What are the animal's weight and height statistics?

_____

2. Does the animal have a protective covering or camouflage? _____

The Ed Emberley Connection © 1992 Fearon Teacher Aids

One Wide River to Cross

PRINTMAKING

Materials:

- Styrofoam meat trays
- construction paper (assorted colors)
- tempera paint
- newspaper
- pencils

Lesson Procedure

1. Discuss how the pictures in *One Wide River to Cross* were made using wooden blocks. Each figure or small grouping was cut on a separate block of wood. The wood was then inked and pressed against sheets of rice paper. Sometimes over fifty impressions had to be made on one single page.
2. Suggest that students create a similar effect by carving designs into Styrofoam meat trays with pencils. Students may want to sketch their ideas on scratch paper before carving them into the Styrofoam sheet. (This is one way to recycle unwanted Styrofoam.)
3. Help students prepare an ink pad by painting a thick patch of tempera paint onto newspaper.
4. Have students press their Styrofoam blocks into the paint. (Applying the paint with a brayer or paintbrush works well also.)
5. Invite students to press the painted Styrofoam blocks onto construction paper. Apply more paint before making another print.

Taking It Further . . .

Students can make stationery or greeting cards using various Styrofoam prints and types and sizes of paper.

• ARK-ITECTS •

Materials:

- drawing paper
- construction paper (assorted colors)
- crayons or markers
- pencils
- scissors
- tape
- glue

Lesson Procedure

1. In cooperative groups of four, invite students to use white drawing paper to sketch blueprints for building a three-dimensional ark from construction paper.
2. After the plan is devised and agreed upon by all group members, encourage the building to begin.
3. For a first attempt, students will be more successful if they limit the size of their ark to one that will fit on a 9" x 12" sheet of construction paper.
4. Give students plenty of time to complete their designs.
5. Display the completed arks on a large table covered with blue paper.

Taking It Further . . .

Students will enjoy comparing several ark stories, such as *Llama and the Great Flood* by Ellen Alexander (New York: Thomas Y. Crowell, 1989), *Rise and Shine* by Fiona French (Boston: Little, Brown & Company, 1989), *The Ark* by Arthur Geisert (Boston: Houghton Mifflin, 1988), *Washday on Noah's Ark* by Glen Rounds (New York: Holiday House, 1985), and *Noah's Ark* illustrated by Jane Ray (New York: Dutton Children's Books, 1990).

The Wing on

This exploration of shape is a wonderful introduction to art. Ed Emberley sees triangles in fishtails and bandanas, rectangles in tin cans and skyscrapers, and circles in drums and umbrellas. He challenges the reader to discover more shapes, too.

Boston: Little, Brown & Company, 1961

a Flea

BOOK REPORTS

Materials:

•worksheet on page 95
•pencils

Lesson Procedure

1. Encourage students to look for both concrete and abstract examples of triangles, rectangles, and circles in the books they are reading.
2. Model the activity using a book you have read to the class with which everyone is familiar. Here are some examples of shapes students might find after reading *Charlotte's Web* by E.B. White (New York: Harper, 1952).

Triangle	Rectangle	Circle
the house roof	Fern's house	rides at the fair
Wilbur's ear	the trough	Charlotte's egg sack
the relationship between Charlotte, Wilbur, and Fern	photographer's camera	Templeton's round trips to the dump
		the life cycle seen in the birth of Charlotte's babies

3. Give students a copy of the worksheet on page 95 and invite them to find shapes in the book they are currently reading. While younger students will more easily find concrete examples, encourage older students to find abstract ideas that can be represented by the shapes.
4. Mount the book reports on a bulletin board entitled, "The Shape of Reading."

Taking It Further . . .

Give the students another worksheet. Invite them to cut out the three shapes and glue them to construction paper. Challenge students to use the shapes to illustrate three features of their books, such as characters, scenes, objects, or concepts. Have students write the title and author of their books on the papers.

The Wing on a Flea

Name _____

Book Title _____
Author _____

Find "shapes" in the book you are reading. Write
your ideas inside the circle, triangle, and rectangle.

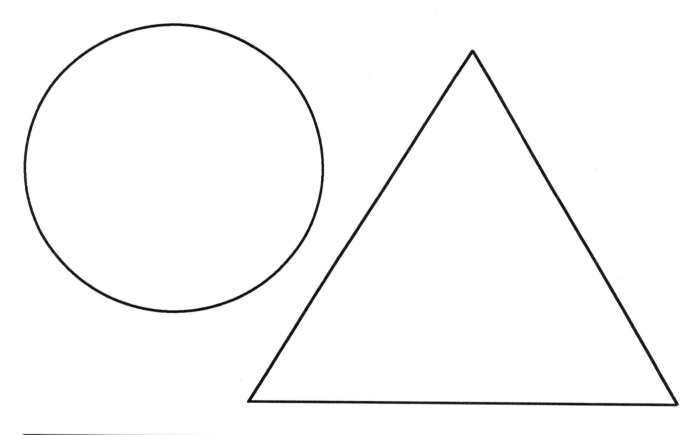

• LISTS •

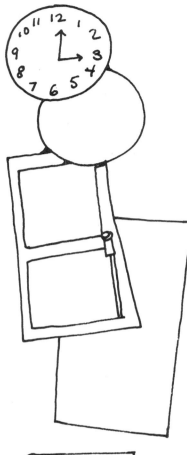

Materials:

•lined paper
•pencils

Lesson Procedure

1. Review with students the shapes used in *The Wing on a Flea* and list on the chalkboard some of the things Ed Emberley made with each shape.
2. Give each student a sheet of lined paper. Have students fold the paper into thirds to make three columns.
3. Have students draw a triangle at the top of one column, a rectangle at the top of the second column, and a circle at the top of the last column.
4. Challenge students to make a list of objects found in the classroom that fit under each shape category.

   Circle—wall clock
   Triangle—pair of scissors
   Rectangle—door

5. Give students the opportunity to share and compare lists.

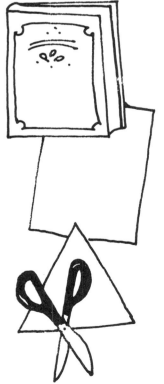

Taking It Further . . .

Play "twenty questions" with shapes in the classroom. A student begins by secretly choosing an object in the room and then giving an initial clue about it, such as "I am thinking of something that is a triangle." Other students ask "yes" or "no" questions to determine what the object is.

The Wing on a Flea